NARADA CONQUERS TEMPTATION

NARADA WAS A DEVARSHI* WHO WAS ALWAYS TRAVELLING ROUND THE WORLD, OFFERING GUIDANCE TO THE DEVOTEES OF THE LORD.

AFTER HAVING GAINED TRUE KNOWLEDGE FROM HIS FATHER, BRAHMA...

...HE TOOK THE VOW OF CELIBACY.

I SHALL NOT MARRY. I WILL SERVE LORD NARAYANA.+

* CELESTIAL SAGE   +VISHNU

NARADA PRACTISED SEVERE AUSTERITIES IN THE HIMALAYAS.

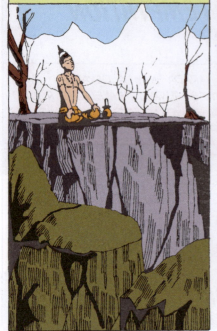

INDRA, KING OF THE DEVAS, BECAME SUSPICIOUS OF NARADA'S MOTIVES. HE SPOKE TO BRIHASPATI * ABOUT IT.

I WONDER WHAT HE IS AFTER.

IT COULD BE YOUR THRONE.

WHAT SHALL I DO? AH! I COULD TEMPT HIM WITH WORLDLY PLEASURES AND MAKE HIM SWERVE FROM HIS PATH.

WITH THIS IN MIND, INDRA SENT FOR KAMADEVA.**

KAMA, I NEED YOUR HELP. YOU MUST MAKE NARADA GIVE UP HIS AUSTERITIES.

I'LL TRY, MY LORD.

* THE ROYAL PRECEPTOR OF THE THE DEVAS ** THE GOD OF LOVE

KAMA CAME TO THE COLD, BARREN SPOT WHERE NARADA WAS SITTING, DEEP IN MEDITATION.

AS HE SHOT THE FIRST ARROW...

...THE SCENE SUDDENLY CHANGED...

... AND A BEAUTIFUL APSARA * APPEARED BEFORE NARADA.

* CELESTIAL DAMSEL

SHE BEGAN TO DANCE BEFORE HIM.

BUT NARADA'S EYES WERE CLOSED TO HER CHARMS.

O SAGE, OPEN YOUR EYES AND BEHOLD YOUR SLAVE.

BUT NARADA HARDLY HEARD HER.

REALISING, THAT SHE WOULD NEVER SUCCEED IN DISTRACTING THE SAGE, THE APSARA LEFT FOR HER HEAVENLY ABODE.

KAMA HAD TO ACKNOWLEDGE DEFEAT.

YOU ARE A GREAT ASCETIC, O SUPREME SAGE! I HAVE FAILED. I BEG TO BE FORGIVEN FOR MY AUDACITY.

NARADA OPENED HIS EYES.

OH, KAMA! WHO SENT YOU HERE?

WHO BUT LORD INDRA!

GO AND TELL INDRA THAT NARADA HAS CONQUERED ALL DESIRES, THAT HE IS ABOVE TEMPTATION.

AND NARADA GLOATED OVER HIS ACHIEVEMENT.

I HAVE DEFEATED KAMA! LORD SHIVA IS NO LONGER THE ONLY CONQUEROR OF THIS INVINCIBLE GOD.*

I MUST GO AND TELL SHIVA ABOUT IT. HE MUST NOW ACCEPT ME AS HIS EQUAL.

* SEE AMAR CHITRA KATHA NO. 506 - SHIVA PARVATI

AT KAILAS, THE ABODE OF SHIVA —

SALUTATIONS TO LORD SHIVA!

COME, NARADA! YOU SEEM PLEASED. WHAT'S THE REASON?

I HAVE CONQUERED KAMADEVA! INDRA SENT HIM TO TEMPT ME. BUT KAMA FAILED!

I AM GLAD TO KNOW THAT! BUT KEEP THE MATTER TO YOURSELF. IN ANY CASE, NEVER BRAG ABOUT IT TO LORD VISHNU!

SHIVA IS JEALOUS OF ME. WHY SHOULDN'T I SPEAK ABOUT MY SUCCESS TO VISHNU? VISHNU, WHO LOVES ME SO DEARLY! I AM SURE HE WILL BE PROUD TO HEAR OF MY VICTORY OVER KAMA.

HE WENT STRAIGHT TO VISHNU'S ABODE.

MAY I PAY MY RESPECTS TO THE GREAT LORD?

COME, NARADA! I AM SO GLAD TO SEE YOU.

YOU WILL BE MORE SO, MY LORD, WHEN YOU LEARN THAT I, YOUR DEVOTEE, HAVE CONQUERED KAMADEVA.

IS THAT SO?

YES, MY LORD! SHIVA IS NO LONGER THE ONLY CONQUEROR OF KAMA. I, YOUR DEVOTEE, AM ABOVE TEMPTATION TOO.

BUT NEVER CEASE TO BE ON YOUR GUARD. YOU NEVER KNOW...

HUH! VISHNU DIDN'T SEEM TOO PLEASED ABOUT MY ACHIEVEMENT EITHER. I AM NO WEAKLING! DOESN'T HE KNOW THAT? WHY SHOULD HE WARN ME TO BE ON MY GUARD?

AS NARADA MOVED ON, SUDDENLY—

WHAT'S THAT? WHAT A WONDERFUL CITY! I'VE NEVER SEEN ONE LIKE IT BEFORE! I MUST VISIT IT.

WHEN HE REACHED THE CITY—

WHO IS THE RULER OF THIS BIG AND CHARMING CITY?

DON'T YOU KNOW? IT BELONGS TO THE GLORIOUS KING, SHEELA-NIDHI. YOU'LL FIND HIM IN HIS PALACE.

HEARING THAT NARADA HAD COME TO VISIT HIM, THE KING CAME OUT TO RECEIVE HIM.

WELCOME, O SAGE! YOU DO US GREAT HONOUR.

JUST THEN THE PRINCESS CAME ON THE SCENE.

THIS IS MY DAUGHTER, SHRIMATI.

WHAT A BEAUTIFUL MAIDEN SHE IS!

AS WAS THE CUSTOM, SHRIMATI BOWED TO THE SAGE.

ARISE, DEAR CHILD. MAY YOU EVER BE HAPPY.

SHE IS READY FOR MARRIAGE. I PLAN TO HOLD A SWAYAMVARA FOR HER SOON.

NARADA GAZED AT THE PRINCESS.

YOUR DAUGHTER IS GODDESS LAXMI*INCAR-NATE. ONE NO LESS THAN HARI⊕IN GLORY AND POWER, SHALL BE HER HUSBAND.

* THE GODDESS OF FORTUNE, VISHNU'S CONSORT ⊕ VISHNU

YOUR WORDS FILL OUR HEARTS WITH JOY. I CANNOT WAIT TO ANNOUNCE THE DATE OF HER SWAYAMVARA.

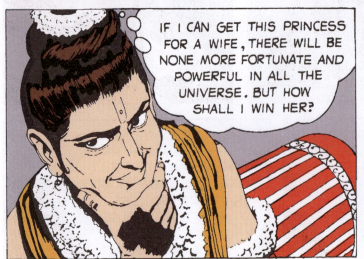

IF I CAN GET THIS PRINCESS FOR A WIFE, THERE WILL BE NONE MORE FORTUNATE AND POWERFUL IN ALL THE UNIVERSE. BUT HOW SHALL I WIN HER?

NARADA PRAYED FERVENTLY TO LORD VISHNU.

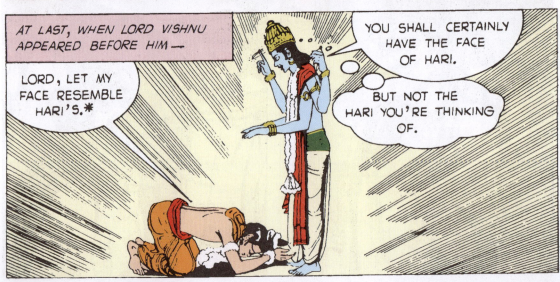

AT LAST, WHEN LORD VISHNU APPEARED BEFORE HIM—

LORD, LET MY FACE RESEMBLE HARI'S.*

YOU SHALL CERTAINLY HAVE THE FACE OF HARI.

BUT NOT THE HARI YOU'RE THINKING OF.

* ANOTHER NAME FOR VISHNU

WHEN NARADA MADE HIS REQUEST HE HAD FORGOTTEN THAT THE WORD HARI ALSO MEANT A MONKEY! AND HE COULD NOT SEE HIS OWN FACE.

HE WENT TO THE SWAYAMVARA HALL FULL OF CONFIDENCE, SURE OF HIS VICTORY.

WHO COULD THAT STRANGE CREATURE BE? A MAN WITH A MONKEY'S FACE! HA! HA!

AND WHAT DOES HE WANT HERE? THE HEART OF SHRIMATI, THE MOST BEAUTIFUL PRINCESS IN THE WORLD?

I HAVE THE HONOUR OF WELCOMING YOU, OUR ROYAL GUESTS, TO THE SWAYAMVARA OF MY DAUGHTER SHRIMATI. SHE SHALL CHOOSE ONE AMONG YOU AS HER HUSBAND. COME MY DAUGHTER, MAKE YOUR CHOICE!

WHAT A DIVINE BEAUTY!

AH! SHE'S COMING TOWARDS ME!

HARDLY NOTICING HIM, SHRIMATI WALKED ON.

SOMEHOW SHE DIDN'T SEE ME. I'LL CROSS OVER TO THE OTHER SIDE. SHE WON'T MISS ME THEN.

WHO ALLOWED HIM IN? HE IS MAKING A NUISANCE OF HIMSELF!

WHERE IS THE LORD OF MY HEART? WHY HASN'T HE COME?

THE NEXT MOMENT—

OH! MY LORD!

AH! THERE HE IS! LORD. WHY DID YOU · · ·

BEFORE HE COULD COMPLETE HIS QUESTION, SHRIMATI HAD GARLANDED VISHNU.

SO THAT WAS IT! HE WANTED HER FOR HIM- SELF. THE TRAITOR!

HE CHARGED FORWARD IN A RAGE.

YOU PROMISED TO GIVE ME YOUR FACE AND GAVE ME A MONKEY'S INSTEAD! WHY?

MY DEAR NARADA, YOU ARE A SCHOLAR OF SANSKRIT. DON'T YOU KNOW, HARI ALSO MEANS MONKEY? YOU DIDN'T SPECIFY WHICH HARI YOU MEANT.

WHO IS THE GREATER DEVOTEE?

I SING THE GLORY OF LORD VISHNU DAY AND NIGHT. WHO CAN BE A GREATER DEVOTEE THAN ME? I WONDER IF THE LORD HIMSELF IS OF THE SAME OPINION.

HE WENT TO VISHNU.

SALUTATIONS TO YOU, MY LORD!

WELCOME, O NARADA! WHAT BRINGS YOU HERE?

I HAVE COME TO ASK YOU A QUESTION.

I KNOW WHAT IT IS. ANYWAY, LET ME HEAR IT FROM YOU.

I HAVE BEEN SINGING YOUR GLORY ALL MY LIFE, EVERY MINUTE OF IT. CAN THERE BE ANYONE MORE DEVOTED TO YOU THAN ME?

IF THAT QUESTION IS TO BE ANSWERED, YOU MUST COME TO EARTH WITH ME.

DISGUISED AS FARMERS, VISHNU AND NARADA CAME TO EARTH AT DUSK AND WALKED TOWARDS A HUT.

OVER THERE, IN THAT HUT LIVES ONE OF MY GREATEST DEVOTEES!

WHOSE DEVOTION IS DEEPER THAN MINE? I WONDER!

DOES HE THINK OF YOU ALL THE TIME AS I DO?

WAIT AND SEE FOR YOURSELF.

HARI, HARI, GOVINDA!

NARAYANA, NARAYANA!

WHERE DO YOU COME FROM? WHAT CAN I DO FOR YOU?

WE WERE ON OUR WAY TO THE CITY. IT'LL SOON BE DARK AND THE FOREST IS INFESTED WITH WILD ANIMALS. WE SEEK SHELTER FOR A NIGHT.

YOU ARE WELCOME TO STAY WITH ME, MY FRIENDS, AND PARTAKE OF WHAT MEAGRE FARE I CAN OFFER YOU.

I AM GRATEFUL TO GOD FOR GIVING ME THIS OPPORTUNITY TO SERVE HIM. PRAISED BE HIS NAME!

THERE ARE TWO GUESTS IN THE HOUSE. PLEASE MAKE SOME EXTRA CHAPATIS*

* UNLEAVENED BREAD

THIS IS ALL THE FLOUR I HAVE, AND THE CHILDREN ARE CLAMOURING FOR MORE FOOD.

NEVER MIND! THE GUESTS MUST HAVE THEIR FILL. MAKE SOME GRUEL FOR THE CHILDREN.

SOON AFTER THEY HAD FINISHED EATING THE CHAPATIS —

HOW CAN THIS SIMPLE HOUSE-HOLDER BE SUCH A GREAT DEVOTEE.

I AM STILL VERY HUNGRY.

THE FARMER WENT TO THE KITCHEN.

IS THERE ANY FOOD LEFT?

NOTHING, EXCEPT THE GRUEL I COOKED FOR THE CHILDREN.

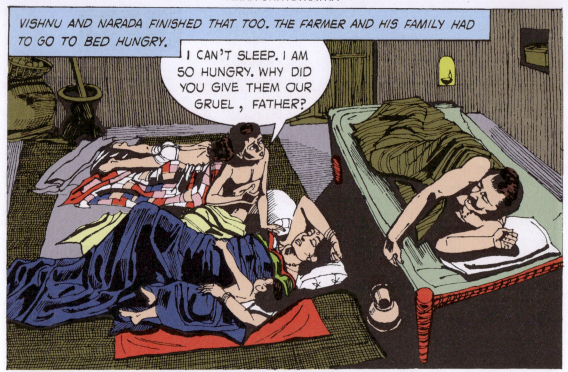

VISHNU AND NARADA FINISHED THAT TOO. THE FARMER AND HIS FAMILY HAD TO GO TO BED HUNGRY.

I CAN'T SLEEP. I AM SO HUNGRY. WHY DID YOU GIVE THEM OUR GRUEL, FATHER?

BECAUSE BY FEEDING A GUEST I AM FEEDING VISHNU HIMSELF.

SEE, NARADA, THE FARMER AND HIS FAMILY HAVE EATEN NOTHING THIS EVENING; AND YET HE SINGS MY GLORY.

THAT'S NOTHING! I HAVE REMAINED WITHOUT FOOD FOR DAYS AND STILL REMEMBERED YOU!

THE NEXT MORNING —

GOVINDA, HARI, HARI! LORD, MAY I ALWAYS HAVE FAITH IN YOU. I SEEK NOTHING ELSE.

PRAISE BE TO HARI, WHO SUSTAINS THE WORLD!

LORD BE PRAISED! FRIENDS, I HOPE YOU SLEPT WELL LAST NIGHT. YOU MAY STAY HERE AS LONG AS YOU PLEASE. I MUST NOW BE OFF TO MY FIELDS.

WE'LL COME WITH YOU, IF YOU DON'T MIND.

21

NARADA AND VISHNU ACCOMPANIED THE FARMER TO HIS FIELD.

HA! HERE WE ARE! I MUST NOW GET DOWN TO WORK, GOVINDA, HARI, HARI.

WHAT A PIOUS MAN YOU ARE! ARE YOU A GREAT DEVOTEE OF THE LORD? YOU KEEP REPEATING HIS NAME.

I REMEMBER HIS GLORIOUS NAME AS OFTEN AS MY WORK PERMITS.

HOW OFTEN WOULD THAT BE?

WELL, I THINK OF HARI AS I GET UP, BEFORE I GO TO BED, AND AS MANY TIMES IN BETWEEN AS MY WORK PERMITS.

I SEE.

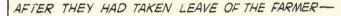

AFTER THEY HAD TAKEN LEAVE OF THE FARMER—

HE THINKS OF YOU AT NIGHT, IN THE MORNING AND A FEW TIMES IN BETWEEN. WHILE I THINK OF YOU ALL THE TIME. AND YET YOU CALL HIM ONE OF YOUR GREATEST DEVOTEES!

YOU'LL SOON SEE WHY, DEAR NARADA.

VISHNU GAVE NARADA A VESSEL FILLED TO THE BRIM WITH OIL.

BALANCE THIS VESSEL ON YOUR HEAD, WALK ROUND THAT HILL AND COME BACK HERE WITHOUT SPILLING A DROP OF THE OIL.

IT WON'T BE EASY, BUT WITH YOUR GRACE IS THERE ANYTHING THAT CANNOT BE ACCOMPLISHED?

AND NARADA SET OFF.

I MUST BE CAUTIOUS LEST THE OIL SHOULD SPILL.

AH! AH! THAT WAS A CLOSE CALL! HAD I SLIPPED, THE OIL WOULD HAVE SPILT. I MUST BE MORE CAREFUL.

WHEN NARADA SUCCESSFULLY COMPLETED THE ROUND—

YOU'RE BACK. GOOD! BUT TELL ME HOW MANY TIMES DID YOU REMEMBER ME DURING THE WALK?

NOT ONCE, I'M AFRAID. HOW COULD I? ALL MY ATTENTION WAS FIXED ON THE OIL AND THE VESSEL!

THAT FARMER HAS HARD WORK TO DO. YET HE REMEMBERS ME — AT LEAST A FEW TIMES. WHILE YOU COULD NOT REMEMBER ME EVEN ONCE!

I CONCEDE IT, MY LORD. THOSE WHO REMEMBER YOU AMIDST WORLDLY CARES ARE WITHOUT DOUBT YOUR GREATEST DEVOTEES.

NARADA ENLIGHTENED

THE CELESTIAL SAGE, NARADA, ONCE CAME TO DWARAKA, TO SEE LORD KRISHNA.

WELCOME, NARADA. WHAT BRINGS YOU HERE?

KRISHNA, I WANT TO KNOW WHAT MAYA* IS? CAN YOU EXPLAIN?

NARADA, MAYA CAN'T BE EXPLAINED. IT HAS TO BE EXPERIENCED, TO BE UNDERSTOOD. COME WITH ME.

BOTH KRISHNA AND NARADA LEFT DWARAKA...

* ILLUSION

...AND KEPT WALKING TILL THEY CAME TO A DESERT.

WHERE ARE WE GOING? HOW CAN I EXPERIENCE MAYA IN A DESERT, KRISHNA?

BE PATIENT, NARADA.

AFTER THEY HAD WALKED A GOOD DISTANCE, KRISHNA SUDDENLY STOPPED.

I CAN'T WALK ANY FURTHER, NARADA. MY THROAT IS PARCHED. TAKE THIS...AND FETCH ME...SOME... WATER.

HOLD ON, KRISHNA. I'LL BE BACK SOON.

NARADA WENT IN SEARCH OF WATER.

IT LOOKS LIKE A SETTLEMENT THERE.

NARADA FOLLOWED THE DAMSEL···

···TO HER HOUSE.

ARE YOU THE MASTER OF THIS HOUSE?

NOT ONLY OF THIS HOUSE BUT ALSO OF THE ENTIRE VILLAGE. WHAT DO YOU WANT, STRANGER?

I SEEK THE HAND OF YOUR DAUGHTER.

WHY NOT? YOU LOOK YOUNG, HEALTHY AND STRONG. BUT··· THE MAN WHO MARRIES MY DAUGHTER MUST STAY IN THIS VILLAGE, IN THIS HOUSE.

IS THAT ALL? I'M WILLING TO ABIDE BY YOUR CONDITION.

ANYTHING TO MAKE THAT GIRL MY WIFE.

THE MARRIAGE SOON TOOK PLACE.

SOON AFTER THE MARRIAGE, THE OLD CHIEFTAIN DIED. NARADA HAD TO ASSUME HIS TITLE AND HIS RESPONSIBILITIES.

I WANT THE WORK FINISHED BY EVENING.

IT WILL BE DONE, MASTER.

NARADA WAS BLESSED WITH FOUR CHILDREN.

FATHER, PUT HIM DOWN AND CARRY ME.

WHEN NARADA WAS AT THE PEAK OF HIS SUCCESS, DISASTER CAME IN THE FORM OF CYCLONIC WINDS, RAIN AND FLOODS.

THE HOUSE WILL SOON BE SUBMERGED! WHAT SHALL WE DO?

FATHER!

NARADA PUT HIS FAMILY INTO A BOAT AND TRIED TO KEEP AFLOAT, ON THE SWIRLING WATERS.

BUT THE BOAT CAPSIZED. NARADA TRIED IN VAIN TO SAVE HIS WIFE AND CHILDREN.

FATHER!

WHERE ARE YOU! DON'T PANIC. I AM COMING!

FATHER!

A HUGE WAVE THREW NARADA ON TO THE SHORE.

MY WIFE GONE! MY CHILDREN DROWNED! HOW CAN I LIVE WITHOUT THEM?

SUDDENLY, HE HEARD A VOICE.

NARADA, I AM THIRSTY. WHERE IS THE WATER?

NARADA TURNED AND BEHELD KRISHNA.

KRISHNA! MY WIFE! MY CHILDREN! BRING THEM BACK TO LIFE.

COME TO YOUR SENSES, NARADA. THERE NEVER WAS ANY WIFE OR CHILDREN. IT WAS ALL MAYA.

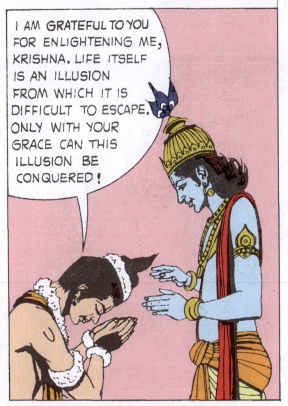

I AM GRATEFUL TO YOU FOR ENLIGHTENING ME, KRISHNA. LIFE ITSELF IS AN ILLUSION FROM WHICH IT IS DIFFICULT TO ESCAPE. ONLY WITH YOUR GRACE CAN THIS ILLUSION BE CONQUERED!

THE ACK QUIZ
EPICS & MYTHOLOGY

1 What is Parashurama's weapon?

2 Who were Krishna's birth parents?

3 Who is the person in the image?

4 Who was his mother?

5 Who was he married to?

6 Who is the woman in the image?

7 She is also known as Jahnavi. Which sage is she named after?

8 Which king brought her down to earth?

9 Manthara was the maid of which queen?

10 Who is Jatayu's brother?